HEALING — MORE OR LESS

by

Jim Cotter

This book of reflections and prayers has been shaped by two concerns. The first is to balance the religious tendency that gives the word "healing" too narrow a meaning—a miraculous moment for individuals. The second is to challenge the view that bodily health is of little importance in the perspective of eternity.

Healing is not just about an individual's physical condition, but has a wide-ranging corporate dimension and spiritual depth. Also, it is not confined to specific incidents or occasions of prayer, but is to be seen in the perspective of a lifetime. And if, in Christian belief, healing is not confined to this life, but ultimately includes death and goes beyond it, yet a healthy flesh-body is a real, if partial, sign of the Commonwealth of God.

Further, in the mid-eighties, the phenomenon of AIDS is showing us that a disease cannot be separated from the social, political, and moral dimensions of the life of a society, nor from the irrational ways in which many people still react to disease. This is heightened when sexuality and blood are two of the issues, when the disease is not curable, and when, under certain circumstances, it can be passed invisibly from person to person. So there is a section in what follows which tries to let the particularities of this crisis concentrate the mind and heart. The crisis also occasioned the drawing on the cover by Peter Pelz: I am grateful to him for permission to reproduce it from "Prayer in the Day" by Jim Cotter and Peter Pelz.

I am also grateful to several people whose thinking has helped me over the years and whose ideas have become inextricably woven with my own. I want especially to acknowledge the writings of Michael Wilson and John V. Taylor (a particular quotation comes from a Church

Missionary Society Newsletter which he wrote 24 years ago), the Prayer Books of the Church of England and the Episcopal Church of the United States of America, and the publications of the Guild of Health. The section on anointing with oil is indebted to a conversation with Alan Harrison.

One or two of the prayers first appeared in compilations under the titles "Prayer at Night" and "Prayer in the Morning".

One particular note of explanation: "Bapu" is an eastern word for "Father", and in its context (and I think in its sense) it combines respect with intimacy.

The last chapter includes material for corporate and individual prayer for healing. It is unlikely that every section will be used on any one occasion. The dots indicate appropriate places for silence and personal detail.

Jim Cotter, January 1987

Dedicated
to the people of the parish of All Saints' Leavesden
who provided the original stimulus for this compilation,
in Lent and Eastertide 1980

CONTENTS

Far More Than Individual Cure:
A Healthy Person,
A Healthy Community,
A Healthy World

A Healthy Person:

The whole of me is being healed,
not merely my symptoms cured.
I experience illness not as an unfortunate incident,
but as a phase of life with its own time and meaning.

I experience the gift of moments of salvation:
the wide open spaces of freedom,
where it is possible to breathe again,
sprung from the trap,
released from every kind of confinement.

I pray and work for the healing of the nations,
for food for the hungry and justice for the oppressed,
for all my neighbours in a global village,
without whose well-being I cannot be completely well.

I am aware that everything that I am and do
contributes to the making of my soul-body,
and the making of the soul-bodies of others,
and the coming to glory of the whole universe,
through everything that is of agony or of ecstasy
in the life of my flesh-body,
that we may be transfigured.

I receive the gift of eternal life,
abiding close to the self-giving love of God,
the love that is not destroyed by death.

A Healthy Community:

We are not afraid of differences,
but are enriched by them.

We do not turn away from defects and handicaps,
distancing ourselves through fear,
but we draw near and touch,
and work with whatever keeps us,
visibly or invisibly handicapped,
from loving one another to completion.

We recognise how the illness of an individual
so often reflects a corporate dis-ease in society:
air pollution, radiation, working conditions, city stress.

We soberly remember that we are relatively well
at other people's expense.

We approach death as a kindly boundary to earthly life,
giving that life both challenge and measure.

A Healthy World:

A world in which we know deeply
that we belong to one another:
there is no place of escape
from the tiresomeness of other people.

A world in which we pray and work
for the well-being of business, factory, farm, bank,
where we search for their meaning and purpose,
where we repent of what goes wrong,
where we act to put things right,
where we celebrate what goes well.

A world in which we are alert to signs of God at work
in the way things are being done,
God striving to transform the realms of this world
into the realm of Christ.

A world in which the work of those involved in public health,
in waterworks, in sewage farms, in canteens, and the like,
is valued and held in high esteem.

A world flowing with milk and honey, with corn, wine, and oil,
where salvation is *not less than* freedom from deprivation.

A world in which there is increasing sensitivity to the poor
and action with them,
in which nations maturely handle
large-scale changes to eliminate poverty,
changes that are political, economic, military.

A world where we become more healed by being prepared
to bear more for the sake of those who are less well.

Is not this the fast that I choose:
to loose the bonds of wickedness,
to undo the thongs of the yoke,
to let the oppressed go free,
and to break every yoke?

Is it not to share your bread with the hungry,
and bring the homeless poor into your house;
when you see the naked to cover him,
and not to hide yourself from your own flesh?

Then shall your light break forth like the dawn,
and your healing shall spring up speedily.

Isaiah 58.6–8

The kingdom of the world has become the kingdom of our Lord
and of his Christ, and he shall reign for ever and ever.

Revelation 11.15b

Healing as a Symbol of Something More:
The Healings of Jesus;
Unusual Healings Now

The Healings of Jesus were symbols,
heralds of a new age,
indicators of the way God wills life to be,
signs of much more than mere cure.
They raised questions:

Do you want to grow in responsibility in life,
do you *want* to be healed?

Do you need to know that you are forgiven?

Is a trusting spirit growing in you—
and in your friends, who may, in faith,
carry you when you are too weak to know or care?

Can you let go of fear and doubt and resentment,
can you bear sorrow and decay,
in the light of belief that death is not the final power?

However raw your life and however much pain you bear,
can you use this very raw material to allow God to shape you,
not for ease, but for glory?

Is your life about being physically well and sleek,
or is your first priority being Christlike—
humble, grateful, trusting, forgiving?

An unusual healing evokes wonder:
"It was so unexpected, such a surprise,
it filled me with joy and gratitude: it was a miracle."
So says the person suddenly cured of a disease,
so says the woman who has given birth after years of hoping.

Let our response be thankfulness to God,
and a deepening of our faith and trust,
and prayer that such events be more everyday.

And let us also reflect:

Much in life that cannot be explained now may be understood in years to come.

God is as much to be praised in the commonplace as in the unusual, as much in the western surgeon's skill as in the psychic surgeon's trance or the healer's hands.

Those with abilities that others cannot grasp, like that of the accountant or the healer, may use that gift either to exercise control and boost their salary or sense of self-importance, dominating others, or to serve the good of others and build up the community.

Even after a marvellous cure, there are challenges to be faced: the healing of the whole personality, and of broken or partial relationships, is a long, deep, and costly process. Faith in God through it all is never easy.

Dramatic healings can be misunderstood: Jesus himself saw the temptation to use such power to stun people into following him. "Turn stones into bread . . . throw yourself off the roof of the Temple." And he realised that the way to the deeper dimensions of healing lies through struggle, weakness, suffering, death. The way of amazing power is too shallow.

Powers More Than We Can Handle:
To Exclude? To Distance? To Include?

To Exclude?

So often we fight to exclude, to banish, to cast out the powers of disease. We use the language of war: heart *attack*, *invading* bacteria, *laid low* by a virus, *anti*-biotics, *bombarded* with rays, *in the grip of* forces I can't control; something *came over me; cast out* the devil, *exorcise* the demon.

We need to be careful about such language, for it is all too easy to exclude the inconvenient, anything or anyone that makes us feel uneasy, to assume that they must be banished or destroyed because they make us feel uncomfortable. We project our own fears on to a large screen, and say that we don't want to see *them*, whether they be the mentally handicapped, the disfigured, the elderly, the person with AIDS.

But is not exclusion *at best* an *emergency* action?

We amputate a leg only when it is absolutely necessary in order to save a person's life.

We put people in prison because we know no more constructive way of righting a personal and social relationship that has gone wrong.

We used to remove part of a person's brain as an attempt to stop particular patterns of behaviour . . . .

We used to burn people at the stake because of their supposed evil or heresy, sometimes saying, This is for the good of your soul . . . .

To Distance?

Sometimes a distancing is necessary, but for the sake of a deeper coming together later, or for the sake of a greater maturity. It can be for our good that we are apart.

Parents and children have to separate, for
> "Selfhood begins with a walking away,
>   And love is proved in the letting go."
>
> C. Day Lewis

Couples may need to separate so that they can learn to grow out of a "love" that has been too much a possessing and being possessed.

Some prayers of "exorcism" have helped a distancing, for example, between living and departed. It is a prayer of letting go, either by the living or by the ancestor.

Some are helped by visualising a compulsion as an "entity" that can be commanded in the name of Christ to leave a person and cause no more disturbance.

To Include?

Prayers of exorcism may look beyond exclusion or distancing to reconciliation and inclusion, e.g.

> In the name of Christ, I bid you depart, [N,] and trouble us no more. Be taken up into the presence of God until such times as we can be reconciled.

> In the name of Christ, come out of darkness into light, [N]; help us to understand you, that we may know your name and nature, striving with you in the love of God, so that you may come to yield your energy in the service of all that is holy.

Yes, there is sometimes chaos inside a person. But much "devilish" behaviour occurs because we have been deeply hurt and desire revenge. We have not yet come to terms with the fact that all of us hurt one another, we hurt especially the very young and vulnerable, and we do not yet realise that blame-throwing is of no use.

The challenge is to understand these threatening powers, to forgive those who have hurt us, and to go through the pain of separation and loneliness, rather than escape from it into compulsion and false solace. If we so accept the challenge, we shall emerge more whole, compulsive behaviour will diminish, and we shall use the energy that has now been "bound" in loving ways, the area of our freedom having been enlarged.

Jesus did not escape *from* crucifixion, but went through it. He did not expel the evil that came at him, but absorbed and transformed it. He *withstood*, *stood under*, understood, enduring as seeing the One who is invisible.

We cannot banish to the "desert" that which is destructive and evil, for in one very small world, what is "desert" to one is "territory" to another. *Together* we are challenged to tackle what is evil.

So often, too, we want to banish parts of ourselves, so unwelcome to the part that is in control and wants to be acceptable and respectable. We condemn and rage against the enemy within, and even for a while may succeed in keeping that enemy out of our own sight and awareness. Yet we are in so much need of our own compassion and patient care, of awareness and acceptance of ourselves.

Awareness in a Nuclear Age

My pact with the Destroyer
was signed before my hands
were old enough to hold a pen.

"Deeply desiring that bonfire—
detonated in the desert of the West
in the Anno Domini of my birth—
to spread and engulf a hated world,
I relish my enemy's holocaust
who is now my neighbour and myself."

"Nonsense, of course we all want peace."

The desire denied yet haunts,
disturbs a dream,
urges in moments of pique,
flashes of prejudice
dismissed as trivial by the conscious mind.

The desire grows,
brushing past me as I press the button
that draws a curtain
and consigns a corpse
to crematorium flames.

The desire reigns:
needles, pellets, triggers, buttons
move closer to my reach.
I look into the Abyss,
see the reflection of my own self-loathing,
and cackle, "Welcome!"

Simple, satisfying, Final Solution.
Auschwitz the curtain raiser
pales to insubstantial ash.

No longer do I say,
"See you tomorrow, D. V."
Rather do I mutter to capricious gods,
"Reagan and Gorbachev permitting,"
not knowing if I will them
to protect or to destroy.

The pact cannot be unmade
until with clear-eyed courage
I dare to dive in dark grey seas,
muddied by an ancient turbulence,
dig out the parchment from the sand,
and let it rise.

I recognise the writing as my own,
unlimited evil in my bland suburban heart,
thirst for revenge against an unknown source of pain.
I weep the cleansing truth that *I* desire these things.

In quietness of tears spent,
I look again into the deep Abyss,
consign the parchment to the flames,
and see them form the Face
that holds me without words.

Marked indelibly by eyes of fierce compassion,
empowered and burning,
stripped of the sentimental mask of cruelty,
I walk in clear-etched gentleness,
with firm and kindly tread on cared-for earth.

4.
Bearing More:
Bearing One Another's Burdens

Some people become voluntary pain-bearers, absorbing the anger and hurt of others, and giving back acceptance and care.

Think of the charge nurse on a hospital ward, bearing the anxiety of the patient, the panic of a mother whose son has had a bad accident, the stress of the staff.

Think of the therapist, who for a while has become the client's hated parent, and who receives the vengeful feelings of the betrayed child, and does not give back further pain.

Think of those on the end of telephones—Samaritans, or the complaints department of a big store or public transport system.

Think of the buddy who is available for the person with AIDS who may have been rejected by family and friends and fellow workers.

These are the ones who refuse to blame-throw, who refuse to scapegoat individuals or minority social groups, who bear the discomfort of a world far from well.

Go deeper still into what healing is all about, and you discover a strange yet creative exchange among those who admit to each other that they are wounded. In the bearing of one another's burdens, in the sharing of one another's pain, we begin to dance.

When we visit the sick, really visit, really being there for the other with the whole of ourselves, we find that we are visiting Christ. To look into gaunt and hollow eyes, full of pain and longing and courage, is to look into the eyes of Christ. *He* is the one who is ill, the one whom we tend, the one who is vulnerable to our blundering.

Together we dance the dance of the crippled, crippled because, however fit and handsome, we are all far from being truly whole, yet a dance because in the midst of suffering we do give each other courage and joy, a sign that indeed one day all shall be well, broken bones shall joy, and with those very wounds we shall find that we have been made whole.

"Surely he has borne our griefs and carried our sorrows;
yet we esteemed him stricken, smitten by God and afflicted.
But he was wounded for our transgressions,
he was bruised for our iniquities;
upon him was the chastisement that made us whole,
and with his stripes we are healed."   [Isaiah 53.4–5]

"Bear one another's burdens,
and so fulfil the law of Christ."   [Galatians 6.2]

"My sorrow cannot be healed, I am sick at heart . . . .
My heart has been crushed, because my people are crushed.
Is there no balm in Gilead? Are there no doctors there?
Why, then, have my people not been healed?
I wish my head were a well of tears,
so that I could cry day and night
for my people who have been killed.   [Jeremiah 8.18,21–9.1]

Alas Yet More:
In a Time of Life-Threatening Epidemic

It is a time of fear, of apprehension,
a fear of pain and disfigurement,
a fear of hateful eyes and deeds of violence,
a fear of the power of those who want
to quarantine, to imprison,
to tattoo with identity marks
(shades of Auschwitz),
a fear of the death-dealing.
There is a tightening,
a pressure on the chest,
a desire for air, for space
beyond the narrow constricted gate.
There is cold fear in a time of tribulation,
a time of the olive press, the winepress,
the crushing of the grapes,
and no guarantee of a good vintage . . . .

Again arises from the heart of suffering the ancient cry,
O God, why? O God, how long?
And the cry is met with silence.
Dare I look steadily at Christ,
at God involved in the isolation and despair,
willing to be contaminated, to be infected,
loving faithfully and in patient endurance,
until all that is being created reaches its final destiny,
in glory, joy, and love?
And yet, why *this* degree of pain?
Why these ever-repeated battles,
with a swathe cut through a generation?
Horrific sacrifice—for what?
Why? Why?

Apocalyptic literature is written in days of crisis,
in a time of judgment,
a time of sifting,
of making clear where people stand.
It is written when there is no sign of deliverance,
no hope,
no meaning:
a day of "the wrath".
It is written at a time of eclipse,
of not knowing,
of learning how to bear a new and impossible burden,
deeper and deeper within us,
not yet able to discern the hand of God.
It is written at a time of being redeemed by fire or fire—
the fire of destruction or the fire of refining?

And is not our present fear of nuclear annihilation,
either suddenly or by seeping radiation,
silent, invisible, all-pervasive,
being projected on to a virus and those who carry it?
Is not this part at least of the reason
for the excessive fear and panic?
Can we allow our terror to surface,
to be acknowledged,
to melt in an incredible leap of faith
in invincible love,
and so choose now to become people
of unprecedented truth, candour, and trust?

AIDS shows up clearly what our attitudes are.
It is forcing us to *choose*,
and the degree of our health is revealed by our response.

Do you punish or embrace a sufferer?

Do you isolate or care?

Are feelings of condemnation evoked in you out of a split-off unconscious, or feelings of compassion out of your struggle to become more whole?

Do you hate yourself the more or do you know yourself more deeply loved?

Do you oversimplify or bear the complexities and the unresolved?

Do you quarantine or touch?

Do you scapegoat the different or welcome their gifts?

Do you reject the disfigured and the dying or do you sit with them in peaceful presence and silent prayer?

Are you withdrawing, afraid of yourself, or does your heart go out to those who suffer?

Donald Nicholl in an address in Holy Week in 1986 observed that if our reaction to something bad happening to another person is one of, "He deserves it," our hearts are still cold and hating. For we have demonised the other and deadened our compassion. We may feel more comfortable with ourselves, but it is a false peace.

Many will fall by the wayside in this crisis
through which the world is passing.
And for those who do fall,
maybe their only choice is *how* to fall,
afraid, or rebellious, or trusting.
Yes, we are angry that such things should happen—
and yet we are aware of so little.
Faith *may* give us a glimpse that we are part
of a greater history that we do not yet see,
part of a greater story.
But this gives no easy certainty.
God does not automatically and immediately
make everything all right.
God does not intervene sporadically,
even as a *benevolent* puppeteer,
but lets be what goes wrong,
suffering and redeeming the consequences
in a love that does not let go.
So when everything is going wrong for us,
at a profound level—
in God—
everything is all right.
Love does not let go—
never, never, never, never, never.
I find I cannot proclaim that loudly and confidently.
I can but whisper it.
I do not have the imperial confidence of a previous century,
not the faith of
"*Firmly* I believe and truly",
but . . . .

Barely I believe yet truly
God is One and God is Three,
God is Love and seen most fully
Hanging from the wintry Tree.

And I trust Creator Spirit
In and through our common life
Weaving threads all torn and broken,
Shaping justice out of strife.

And I cherish—with due patience—
For the sake of God alone,
Words and Folk of Inspiration,
And the Sacraments Christ's own.

I embrace the Law of Loving,
Dying to possessive need,
Risen with Christ, though crushed by winepress,
Into spacious glory breathed.

Written for an evening of
meditation in support of
The Parsonage, the Episcopal
Church's outreach to the gay
constituency in San Francisco:
November 1986

"We must accept the fact that this is an age in which the cloth is being unwoven. It is therefore no good trying to patch. We must, rather, set up the loom on which coming generations may weave new cloth according to the pattern God provides."

[Gilbert Shaw]

We need to beware of importing meaning where AIDS is concerned. We want order, we want to make sense of what is happening. But it is too easy to introduce metaphors of immediate religious significance. All that is written in these particular pages is tentative. We may have to live with the fact that we can discern *no* meaning in this disease.

I wouldn't know what to say.
I knew him in his prime,
lively, intelligent, witty, loving:
you felt encouraged by simply being with him.
He was even eloquent about the problem of suffering.
Now you can hardly recognise him.
And he can't speak.
A stroke was it? Or a virus? Or a tumour?
What does the label matter?
The *person* we loved,
we looked up to,
is reduced to this.
It seems so pointless.
It *is* so pointless.
Both of us are struck dumb.
So much for the wisdom of old age,
the elders sitting in the city square.
This is the reality,
incontinent and helpless in an oblong ward.

No meaning here, no purpose.
No gain that we can see,
either for him,
or for those who care for him.
Just this hard implacable *fact* of his suffering.
He's not hurting instead of someone else—
no courageous witness of the prison camp.
He's not hurting on behalf of others,
showing them that there is a way through . . . .
Useless, useless anguish . . . .
Useless?
Is this where we go wrong?
Are we so attuned to the values of the age
that we judge only by results,
only by usefulness?
Rendered speechless by any "thusness" that will not budge?
Beyond our power to produce results?
"I'm afraid there's no more that we can do."
We interpret this as doom, as sentence of death.
But maybe that's a sign—
being useless.
For if I'm loved in that precise condition,
not respected,
not needed,
not able to give,
then love might be,
might be,
the power that moves the universe.

There is no straightforward connection in terms of cause and effect between acts of wrongdoing and disease. Yet there *is* a connection: disease is one of the manifestations of "sin", in this sense: the tendency of the whole of life to be organised for decay, disaster, destruction, disfigurement, death, together with the self-devouring desire for these things which each human being knows something of.

So, when we examine the context of our experiences, we do perceive some degree of connection
    between sexual activity and disease,
    between coal mining and lung complaints,
    between business pursuits and heart attacks,
    between anxiety and ulcers,
    between radiation and pollution and cancers.

There is no simple cause and effect, but the diseases are signs of the corporate gonewrongness, a pervasive disorientation in which all of us are caught. It is impossible, unhelpful, and cruel to apportion individual blame, but certain states of mind and certain ways of acting can make us more prone to certain kinds of disease.

If diseases are, as some would claim, God's wrathful thunderbolts, then we have to admit that the targeting is inaccurate. For drug traffickers and arms traders flourish, lesbian women are least likely to contract AIDS, and children develop the disease. No, God makes his sun to rise on the evil and on the good, and sends rain on the just and on the unjust.   [Matthew 5.45]

God does not run the world by *our* ideas of reward and punishment. Health and vigour do *not* correlate well with virtue and innocence. And if health does not prove goodness, affliction does not prove wickedness.

We do the blaming of the "victims"—
   "The unemployed are lazy." (Has laziness all that
   dramatically increased in the past ten years, and more
   so in the north of Britain than in the south?)
   "The cancer patient ate the wrong foods."
   "The rape victim enticed the rapist."
We feel more secure by trying to shift the blame, and we bargain with God—He'll be good to us if we keep the rules.

All are in need of repentance, *without* exception. No-one is without sin, no-one dare cast a stone. The ones who are judged most severely in the Gospels are the hypocritical, the self-righteous, and the merciless. Disease therefore is not a punishment but a challenge we all face among the myriad other opportunities of our lives, to make of those lives something better.

If we particularly sense that we belong together when we exchange in an intimate way fluids, energy, stuff, we may overdo it. We may try to take in too much, like trying to take in too much information, or trying to get to know too many people. The organism cannot cope: it tries to expel, because there is too much to absorb, process, and change. The exposure may sometimes be too much for the system, there may be an immune overload, and consequently breakdown.

How much, then, can we "host", can we "carry"? We already carry within us much that is potentially lethal, including parasites, and cancerous cells. How much are we challenged to bear, to contain, even to care for and transform some minute entity in the life of the universe that is wild, retrograde, and on the loose? It may be that those most fitted to be "hosts", who come at least to an accommodation with the virus, will prove to be those most fitted to survive. And this may be linked to a whole range of issues connected with health and well-being, issues of diet, physical movement and relaxation, meditation, contemplation, sensitising of touch.

To a virus:

If I have to carry you for the rest of my life,
if I am to be a carrier,
to carry you as part of the burden of the world,
then I must have no inner attitude, no outer action,
that allows you to reflect your attitude and action,
thus increasing your power and urge to destroy
at the biochemical, cellular level of the organism
that is my flesh-body self.
If each person is a universe in miniature,
you, and viruses like you, may be in each of us always.
However much you are held at bay,
your power of destruction lurks.

We cannot expel, conquer, defeat, or destroy you.
We belong together,
we die or live together,
are bound hellward or heavenward together.
I may indeed have to say to you,
"Hold your distance,
Stay in your own place."
I may have to bind you.
But I can create the message, the reality even,
that will make you realise there is nothing for you here.
Perhaps you are open to change,
to mutation, to transformation.
Perhaps you may become my ally,
to the purpose of a greater good.
And even if you take over and run riot,
multiplying and destroying the flesh-body,
you cannot destroy me.
In yourself, you are power without love,
and love will triumph over mere power.
Love can take you and calm you and transform you.
All will serve the purpose of love,
even that which as yet has no meaning,
however much pain there may be on the way.
I may become grotesque and faded as flesh-body,
but whenever I live and act
with courage, faith, compassion and love,
something else is taking shape,
a more complex, subtle, soul-body,
which will emerge fully only when I die . . . .

We are all incredibly fragile and vulnerable.
Each of us has a lost child within.
Look into the eyes of the suffering man or woman,
and see the grief, pleading, fear, courage, anger.
How can you not show compassion?
[Dear God, may this disease bring out in us a new tenderness,
especially for the ones we are tempted to despise.]
If you are without sin—sexual or otherwise—
then throw the stones:
otherwise, give to each and all
the respect they are due through simply being human.

Being weak is not the end of our influence.
We may indeed be a weak spot, a powerless place,
but this may be the exact point
through which mercy can flow into our lives
and into the lives of those with whom we have to do.
If others sense that we know deeply
the trials of suffering and of dying,
they will beat a path to our door,
and will find for themselves some measure of healing.
We shall indeed be "priests",
living at the centre of sacrifice,
the utter giving upon which the world depends for everything.

There is another side to a new disease which is not publicly obvious nor glamorous, and which involves a humble sitting before the facts. And that is the painstaking, laborious, detailed search for a cure, for a vaccine; it is mostly hidden unsung drudgery and tedium.

But a discovery might mean that we shall have also found a way to cure the common cold and 'flu . . . . Thank God for the gift of skills to probe the mysteries of the universe . . .

Another part of the total healing is the facing of truths, even of simple information, that has been hidden by fear and taboo. There is an insistent pressure now to de-mystify sex. Honesty and clarity have an opportunity to surface where there has been too much denial and ignorance.

There is a new clarity, too, about the questions we need to ask about the best ways of becoming whole through our relationships:

How can the strength of the erotic nourish healing and growth between two people?

What kinds of touch will best heal, will help to make love, between these two people now?

What forms of relationship best enable delight, pleasure, enjoyment?

How can the sexual be connected with the meaning of a relationship?

Why do we draw close, how do we draw close, and with what result?

Is not the end celebration, which has no end?

Statements towards the healing of sexual wounds,
and towards freedom from compulsive behaviour:

Thank you, God, for such athletic beauty, even if the psalmist said
you take no delight in anyone's legs.

And I let go, laying quietly on one side the spirit of possessiveness,
and saying with William Blake,
"He who kisses a joy as it flies
Lives in eternity's sunrise."

The next person who passes me in the street is just as much loved by
God as that stunner.

Let thoughts drop into the heart.
Let desires rise into the heart.
Let love spread through the heart.

Breathe into your loneliness and go deep,
and then move gently into the next event.

Laugh at yourself long and out loud.

If other feelings arise, grief, fear, anger,
express them with noise and movement.
Ask somebody to be with you as you do this,
a person who will simply receive you and your feelings together,
without comment.

Cherish your flesh-body.

All these will never be enough to assuage all the pain. Simply bear
with whatever pain that will not shift. There may be no meaning yet.

Because of the letting go of self
that can happen at the height of orgasm,
there is a hint of death in sexual activity.
And now that hint is shouting.
Physically or psychologically,
AIDS is omnipresent where sex is concerned.
It nudges us to come to terms with death.
It reminds us that there are limits
to the satisfaction that comes through sexual intercourse.
Within it there always seems the desire for more—
both in terms of repetition
and in terms of deeper and more lasting union.
Sex never yields all that it promises.
The challenge is to be glad for what it does yield,
and also to acknowledge the gap and live in its tension,
with its reminder that all our unions are transient.

And the opportunity is given to get to know the "root or depth in thee
from whence all thy faculties come forth as lines from a centre, or as
branches from the body of a tree. This depth is called the centre, the
fund, or bottom of the soul." [William Law]

"Such is the deep Christ-Self at the core of us,
the realm of abundant life,
the indestructible deep centre that never gives way,
the small seed which will become the great tree,
the leaven transforming the lump, the eye of the soul,
the ground of being, the heart, the transcendent self,
the extreme point at which God touches us." [Evelyn Underhill]

A Psalm based on Psalm 6

Hideous afflictions of a turbulent age—
virus, cancer, thrombosis, ulcer—
warheads in the fluids of my being:
I am caught in a world that is twisted,
trapped in its web of corruption,
tempted to blame my ills on to "them",
tempted to turn the hatred within.
All together we are hard pressed by discord,
carriers of disease, injectors of poison,
all are victims of our malice and fear.
Paralysed, depressed, we cannot move,
spun in the vortex of death.
Distressed in the very depths of our being,
bones shaking, cells mutating,
we are almost in despair.
In your mercy and grace set us free!
Refine us in the Fire of your Love!
Our cry is of hope, yet struggling with doubt,
a stammer gasping for breath in the night.
How long, O God, how long?

O God, turn your face to me, save my life:
deliver me in the endurance of Love,
ease the burden of guilt and of pain,
let me know the grace of your presence,
now in this life and through the shades of the grave.

I am weary with my suffering,
every night I flood my bed with tears,
I drench my couch with my weeping,
my eyes waste away out of grief,
I grow weak through the weight of oppression.

You that work evil and seek to destroy,
loosen your grip, away from my presence.
For God has heard the sound of my weeping,
forgives me with delight and lightens my gloom.
The destroyers will be ashamed and sore troubled,
trembling, they will be stripped of their power,
no longer able to harm.

And no, I will not gloat or hate,
in the Love of God I will hold on to you yet.
In the anger and hope of the wrath of our God,
come to the place of repentance and mercy.

And you, silent virus, invisible, malignant,
bound up with my bodily being,
are you an enemy that I can befriend,
or at least contain in a place of your own—
your power to harm taken away,
brought with us to the glory of God?

A Psalm based on Psalm 22

My God, my God, why have you forsaken me?
Why are you so far from helping me,
from the sound of my groaning?
O my God, I cry in the daytime,
but you do not hear me.
I howl in the watches of the night,
but I find no rest.

Yet still you are the holy God,
whom Israel long has worshipped.
Our ancestors hoped in you,
and you rescued them.
They trusted in you,
and you delivered them.
They called upon you;
you were faithful to your covenant.
They put their trust in you
and were not disappointed.

But as for me,
I crawl the earth like a worm,
despised by others,
an outcast of the people.
All those who see me laugh me to scorn:
they make mouths at me,
shaking their heads and saying,
"He threw himself on God for deliverance:
let God rescue him then,
if God so delights in him."

You were my midwife, O God,
you drew me out of the womb.
I was weak and unknowing,
yet you were my hope,
even as I lay close to the breast,
cast upon you from the days of my birth.
From the womb of my mother
to the dread of these days
you have been my God,
never letting me go.

Do not desert me,
for trouble is hard at hand,
and there is no one to help me.
Wild beasts close in on me,
narrow-eyed, greedy and sleek.
They open their mouths and snarl at me,
like a ravening and a roaring lion.

My strength drains away like water,
and all my bones are out of joint.
My heart also in the midst of my body
is even like melting wax.
My mouth is dried up like a potsherd,
and my tongue cleaves to my gums.
My hands and my feet are withered,
you lay me down in the dust of death.

The huntsmen are all about me:
a circle of the wicked hem me in on every side,
their dogs unleashed to tear me apart.
They have pierced my hands and my feet—
I can count all my bones—
they stand staring and gloating over me.
They divide my garments among them,
they cast lots for my clothes.

The tanks of the mighty encircle me,
barbed wire and machine guns surround me.
They have marked my arm with a number,
and never call me by name.
They have stripped me of clothes and of shoes,
and showered me with gas in the chamber of death.

I cry out for morphine but no one hears me.
Pinned down by straitjacket I scream the night through.
I suffocate through panic in the oxygen tent.
Sweating with fear, I await news of my doom.

No one comes near without their face masked,
no skin touches mine in a gesture of love.
They draw back in terror, speaking only
in whispers behind doors that are sealed.

Be not far from me, O God:
you are my helper, hasten to my aid.
Deliver my very self from the sword,
my life from the falling of the axe.
Save me from the mouth of the lion,
poor body that I am, from the horns of the bull.

I will declare your name to my friends:
in the midst of the congregation I will praise you.
We stand in awe of you and bow before you,
we, the seed of Jacob, the descendants of Israel,
we glorify and magnify your name.

For you have not shrunk in loathing
from the poor in their affliction.
You have not hid your face from them,
but when they called to you, you heard them.

My praise is of you in the great congregation.
My vows I will perform in their sight.
We shall praise you with thanksgiving and wonder.
We shall share what we have with the poor:
they shall eat and be satisfied,
a new people, yet to be born.
Those who seek you shall be found by you:
they will be in good heart for ever.

So shall my life be preserved in your sight,
and my children shall worship you:
they shall tell of you to generations yet to come;
to people yet to be born
they shall declare your righteousness,
that you have brought these things to fulfilment.

So let all the ends of the world remember
and turn again to their God.
Let all the families of the nations worship their Creator.
For all dominion belongs to you,
and you are the Ruler of the peoples.

Coda

And can those who are buried give you worship,
those ground to the dust give you praise?
Will nothing be left but the wind and the silence,
a dead earth, abandoned, forgotten?

But you are a God who creates out of nothing,
you are a God who raises the dead,
you are a God who redeems what is lost,
you are a God who fashions new beauty,
striving with the weight of your glory,
bearing the infinite pain.

The footfalls of faith may plod through our days,
God's gift of a costly and splendid enduring.
We remember your deliverance of your people of old,
we remember the abundance of the earth you have given us,
we remember the care and compassion of folk,
we remember your victory of long-suffering love.

The power of the powers is but a feather in the wind!
Death is transfigured to glory for ever!

6

Toward Prayer for Healing

God promises to make whole: God is faithful.

God wants us to grow to maturity despite our not always being cured, and God seeks our willing co-operation.

God's love is already at work within us, for we are being created in God's image, however marred.

With our co-operation, by stillness or skill, by means known or means not understood, God shares in human lives for their healing.

Nothing can separate us from the Love-Presence of God.

The Love of God strives to transform all evil and pain.

There is prayer in the rage of one in great pain and in the one who sits silently with another in great pain.

There is prayer in urgent and heartfelt asking, crying, and hammering at heaven's door, expectant of a response.

There is prayer in offering pain in patience and perseverance, gently pressing into the grain of that pain, yielding to its truth.

There is prayer in the exchange of bearing one another's burdens.

An answer to prayer may be given, even if it is not exactly what we prayed for.

Pray for courage to face whatever blocks God's healing work in us.

God's final purposes are known only *through* the grave and gate of death.

The goal of healing is the glorification of the universe.

Pray for graciousness, truth, goodness, love, beauty, peace, Christlikeness, even in the midst of grotesque disfigurement. The disfigured *will* be transfigured.

7

Praying for Healing:
Individual and Corporate Prayer

A Ministry of the People

The ministry of healing is a gift given to the whole people of God. Some may have particular gifts to exercise in that setting, but no gift is to be exercised in a quirky, bizarre, or individualistic way. The pointed question for any community to ask is this:

> Are we a body of people among whom those who are dis-eased will find healing, or is our common life in such disarray that we shall block and hinder that healing?

[In what follows 'A' may be, in different circumstances, minister, priest, leader, fellow pilgrim, and 'B' may be penitent, congregation, fellow pilgrim(s). Most groups and congregations will find it typically (but not necessarily universally) fitting for 'A' to be a person who is recognised as representing and embodying that group or congregation.]

While Preparing for a Service to Begin

A time to align oneself to the love of God within and beyond, to become aware of those praying around . . . .

A time to relax and become still . . . .

Stretch . . . Shake . . . Settle . . . .

Sit with back straight up and down
and with both feet on the ground . . . .

Breathe out gently and a long way,
and then simply let the air in . . . .

Relax into any aches and pains . . . .

No strain . . . Relax . . . Let be . . . .

Bring a word to mind—Peace, Healing, Spirit . . . .
Bring a picture to mind—Running Water, Wide Ocean,
Caring Hands . . . .

Abide in the Presence . . . .

Living Loving God, our Father and Mother,
the Source of life and health, of strength and of peace:
show us the Way, the Truth and the Life;
take from us all that hinders the flow of your Spirit;
with hands of compassion wash away our sin and our fear,
our resentment and our hardness of heart;
enable us to become centred and still,
aware of your Presence, here, now,
to heal, to redeem, to transform . . . .
We pray in the Spirit of Jesus Christ our Saviour.

Thanksgiving and Confession: The Ministry of Reconciliation

[Individual and corporate confession and forgiveness are part of the releasing of folk from the gnawing-nibbling of guilt and memories. Although there is no simple and direct causal link between sin and suffering, they overlap as part of the world's gonewrongness, and we grow in grace only by taking responsibility for our contribution to that gonewrongness. Forgiveness of sin is one of the dimensions of healing and reconciliation. In the service of Holy Communion they lead directly to the gifts of peace and gratitude: the Sharing of the Peace and the Eucharistic Prayer.]

The Ministry of Reconciliation for an Individual

A   The Spirit of the Living God be with you.

B   The Peace of Christ dwell in your heart.

A & B   From the deep places of my soul I praise you, O God:
           I lift up my heart and glorify your holy name.
           From the deep places of my soul I praise you, O God:
           how can I forget all your goodness towards me?
           You forgive all my sin, you heal all my weakness,
           you rescue me from the brink of disaster,
           you crown me with mercy and compassion.
           You are full of forgiveness and grace,
           endlessly patient, faithful in love.
           As vast as the heavens are in comparison with the earth,
           so great is your love towards those who trust you.

           Holy God, Creator and Sustainer of the world,
           Holy and Utterly Loving,
           we give you thanks and praise.

B   Eternal God, Giver of all good gifts,
I your friend and servant
now give you humble and hearty thanks
for all your goodness and lovingkindness
to me and to all folk.
I bless you for my creation, preservation,
and all the blessings of this life.

Especially do I thank you for . . . .

Above all do I thank you for your great love
in the redeeming of the world
by our Saviour Jesus Christ,
for the means of grace
and for the hope of glory.

And I ask of you,
give me that due sense of all your mercies
that my heart may be unreservedly thankful,
and that I show forth your praise,
not only with my lips but in my life,
by giving up myself to your service,
and by walking before you
in holiness and righteousness all my days;

through Jesus Christ my Redeemer,
to whom with you and the Holy Spirit,
be all honour and glory,
world without end. Amen.

A   For God's gift of you to us,
for all that you are and all that you give,
I too thank and praise our faithful Creator.

A & B In your great goodness, O God, have mercy upon me,
in the cascading of your compassion
sweep away my offences.
Wash me thoroughly from my wickedness,
and cleanse me from my sin.
For I acknowledge my fault,
my sin confronts me all the day long.

Holy God, Holy in Refining and Mercy,
Holy and Utterly Loving,
have mercy upon us.

B Pray for me, a sinner.

A May the piercing light of Christ
illuminate your heart and mind,
that you may remember in truth
all your sins and God's unfailing mercy.
For we remember, O God,
how much you love us and all the world;
you have given yourself to us in Jesus Christ,
that we might not perish
but have abundant and eternal life.

B Faithful Creator, Abba, Bapu,
you formed me from the dust in your image,
and you redeemed me from sin and death
through the living, dying, and rising of Christ.
Through baptism you accepted me, cleansed me,
and gave me new life.
You called me to your service and friendship.
But I have wounded your love and marred your image.
I have wandered far in a land that is waste.
Especially do I confess to you, dear God,
and to my sisters and brothers, your People . . . .

Therefore, dear God,
from these sins
and those I cannot now remember
I turn to you in sorrow and repentance.
Receive me in your mercy
and restore me to the blessed company
of your faithful people.

A   May God in mercy receive your confession of sin
and your repentant heart and will.
May God strengthen you in the ways of love and truth.
May God keep you in eternal life.

Our Saviour Jesus Christ,
who has given the power of forgiveness
to the People of God, the Church,
to absolve all sinners who truly repent
and believe in the Gospel
of total and unconditional Love,
of his great mercy forgive you your sins;

[either] and by the authority of Christ
committed to me through his People
and in their name,
I absolve you from all your sins,
in the name of God,
Creator, Redeemer, Sanctifier.

[or] be assured that you are forgiven,
forgiven by Christ,
forgiven by your fellow-pilgrims,
released from all that hurts you.

B   Amen. Thanks be to God.

A   Do you gladly give yourself again to Christ,
to follow the Narrow Way that leads to life,
and to keep your eyes fixed on Christ,
who is the goal and the glory?

B   I do.

A   Will you, in the strength of God's forgiveness of you,
seek to be reconciled with those
who have sinned against you,
and where that is not now possible,
will you keep open a forgiving heart and will?

B   I will.

A   Abide in peace.
God has put away all your sins.
You are restored to the People of God.
Rejoice and be glad.

B   Alleluia.
Thanks be to God.

The Ministry of Reconciliation among the Whole Body

A   The Spirit of the Living God be with you.

B   The Peace of Christ dwell in your heart.

A   Let us be thankful for all that has been
and for all that shall be,
for life itself and for one another,
for God's love for us, unbounded and eternal . . . .

B   Holy God, Creator and Sustainer of the world,
Holy and Utterly Loving,
we give you thanks and praise.

A   Let us go deep into silence,
in gratitude and trust . . . .

        [A time of silence follows]

A & B Eternal God, Giver of all good gifts,
we your friends and servants
now give you humble and hearty thanks
for all your goodness and lovingkindness
to us and to all folk.
We bless you for our creation, preservation,
and all the blessings of this life,
but above all for your inestimable love
in the redemption of the world
by our Saviour Jesus Christ,
for the means of grace
and for the hope of glory.

And we ask of you,
give us that due sense of all your mercies
that our hearts may be unreservedly thankful,
and that we show forth your praise,
not only with our lips but in our lives,
by giving up ourselves to your service,
and by walking before you
in holiness and righteousness all our days;
through Jesus Christ our Redeemer,
to whom with you and the Holy Spirit,
be all honour and glory, world without end. Amen.

A   We grieve and confess
A & B   that we hurt and have been hurt
to the third and fourth generations,
that we are so afraid of pain
that we shield ourselves
from being vulnerable to others,
and refuse to be open and trusting as a child.

A   Abba, Bapu, close your eyes to our sins,
B   we who have wounded your love.
A   Refine us with the fire of your Spirit,
B   cleanse us with springs of living water.
A   Save us with words of forgiveness and peace,
B   make us whole, steadfast in spirit.
A   Broken are our bones, yet you can heal us,
B   and we shall leap for joy and dance again.

A & B   Holy God, Holy in Refining and Mercy,
Holy and Utterly Loving,
have mercy upon us.

A   Abba, Bapu, forgive, renew, empower us,
as a pledge of our maturing
and a foretaste of the freedom
of the whole creation.

B   Thanks be to God,
who accepts us, forgives us and heals us,
through the crucified and risen Jesus,
who absorbs our sin and pain
in an all-embracing love,
overcoming evil with good.

A   Our Saviour Jesus Christ,
who has given the power of forgiveness
to the People of God, the Church,
to absolve all sinners who truly repent
and believe in the Gospel
of total and unconditional Love,
of his great mercy forgive you your sins;

[either] and by the authority of Christ
committed to me through his People
and in their name,
I absolve you from all your sins,
in the name of God,
Creator, Redeemer, Sanctifier.

[or] be assured that you are forgiven,
forgiven by Christ,
forgiven by your fellow pilgrims,
released from all that hurts you.

B   Amen. Thanks be to God.

A   May we forgive one another in the forgiveness of God,
and greet one another in peace.

Speaking with Tongues

"Whether for the individual who is too exhausted to pray or at a loss for words, or the group that is much despised by the verbalisers and dare not be articulate, speaking in tongues is profoundly therapeutic . . . . Need is met. Unconscious tensions are released. Loneliness is appeased. Sickness is healed. Uncertainties about the future are resolved. Inarticulate weakness finds expression.

" 'Whether it exists among the agricultural workers of Chile, the Indians of Argentina, the proletariat of North America, the masses of African cities, the gypsies of France, the members of Swedish trades unions, or the poor in Britain, the function of the Pentecostal movement is to restore the power of speech, and to heal them from this terror of the loss of speech . . . .'

"All the Spirit's gifts are wonderful; all are marked by a certain spontaneity; but none is meant to be weird. They are incalculable, they are corporate. Christian healing is essentially the gift, not of particularly endowed individuals, but of the Spirit-filled community."

[John V. Taylor, quoting Walter Hollenweger]

A Litany

Response: Healing Spirit, set us free.

From wearisome pain . . . .
From the sharp sword of agony . . . .
From burdens too great to bear in love for others . . . .
From guilt and regret about times past . . . .
From fearful memories . . . .
From anxiety and fear for the future . . . .
From the grip of compulsions . . . .
From pride, greed, and bitterness . . . .
From illusion, lying, and pretence . . . .
From the depths of despair . . . .

Response: Spirit of God, make us whole.

Through the ministry of those who care for the sick and seek
    to heal . . . .
Through the ministry of families and companions, and fellow
    friends of God . . . .
Through the ministry of those who serve the public health . . . .
Through the ministry of listening and of presence . . . .
Through the bearing of one another's burdens . . . .
Through the ministry of counselling and therapy . . . .
Through the ministry of prayer and sacrament . . . .
Through our expectant hearts and open minds . . . .
Through bringing our wills into harmony with your loving
    purpose . . . .
Through our joy in being the friends of God . . . .
In the hour of our dying . . . .
In the transfiguring of evil and pain . . . .

The creation will be set free from bondage to decay,
and obtain the glorious liberty of the children of God.

The Lord's Prayer

Beloved Abba,
our Father and Mother,
in whom is heaven,
hallowed be your name,
followed be your royal way,
done be your will and rule,
throughout the whole creation.

With the bread we need for today,
feed us.
In the hurts we absorb from one another,
forgive us,
In times of temptation and test,
strengthen us.
From trials too great to endure,
spare us.
From the grip of all that is evil,
free us.

For you reign in the glory
of the power that is love,
now and for ever.
Amen.

Deliverance

[A ministry of deliverance can help the process of loosening from deep-rooted compulsions or the incessant presence of a person from whom we should be separated. It can focus on God some of the painstaking uncovering of the past that emerges in counselling and therapy.]

People of God,
within us and among us and through the world,
there are many powers of dis-ease which hold us in their grip.
They trouble us, distract us, wound us.
They go by many names: greed, pride, loneliness;
fear, rage, grief; pain, death, evil . . . .
some known in the secret places of our hearts,
some as yet unknown to us,
some greater in strength
than any one of us can bear alone . . . .

Let us be silent awhile
and pray in the name of God,
Liberator, Redeemer, Healer,
revealed to us in Jesus of Nazareth . . . .

[A period of silence]

May we seek to understand and withstand these powers,
to know their name and nature,
that they may cease their hold on us,
and be transformed by the power of that Love
that is deeper than the deepest pain,
that we may be freed to be the friends of God.

A Prayer Focussing on the Needs of a Particular Person

In the name of Jesus Christ,
come out of darkness into light. [N.] *
help us to understand and withstand you,
that we may know your name and nature,
that you may wound us no more,
that you may yield your energy in the service of God.

And where through lack of prayer or fasting
through weak will or fainthearted love,
through fear of your destructive power,
we cannot yet be reconciled,
leave us be,
depart to the place
where we must all one day face
the refining fire and living flame
of the Love of God.

---

* *It may be appropriate to name what is troubling
a person, e.g. spirit of revenge.*

The Laying on of Hands

[Think of the ways in which hands heal:

they can comfort and soothe;

they can touch a person wracked with pain in such a way as brings relief;

they can massage away tensions in the muscles and help to harmonise and order the energies of the body;

there are those whose hands radiate a healing warmth and energy in ways we barely understand;

hands can be a sacramental means of building one another up in the love, joy, and peace of God.

When hands are laid on a sick person in church it is usually by those who represent and lead the Christian community, together with those whose special care the work of healing is. Like all such acts, it is done on behalf of everyone, not instead of them. There is no reason at all why anyone should not lay hands on any other who wishes it, in a gesture of prayer and support, of healing and blessing; and there are some who have a particular gift of healing which can be exercised in a one-to-one way, in a context of continuing pastoral care. In church we demonstrate publicly that healing is one of the major concerns of the Christian community: the public moment focuses that concern, all of which is offered to God for blessing.

Further, since this is the work of the whole community, and since we are bound up with one another in our disease and our healing, I think there is something to be said for the old custom of receiving the laying on of hands on behalf of someone you know who, for example, may be ill in hospital a long way away.

Some years ago, Bob Lambourne made the suggestion that at a
Communion Service which included prayer for healing, the "walking
wounded" and their families (and friends) might at the Offertory bring
to the altar the wine, that our pain might be presented to God for its
transforming. The doctor, the nurse, the health visitor, they might bring
the water, the cup of water that symbolises the response of the
community in care. And those who visit the sick might bring the bread,
symbol of all the nourishing and feeding that we can do for one
another.]

Prayer of Preparation

Blessed are you, eternal God,
Source of all healing,
you have given us the means
by which you make your creatures whole,
our presence and our skills,
our understanding of your laws
and our humility before the unknown,
our words and our hands,
medicines that soothe and cure,
machines that aid our work.
We give ourselves to you:
empty us of all that hinders the flow
of your healing Spirit.
Take our hands and our lives
that we may live in your image
and reflect your glory.

In the name of God,
who is great and good and love,
in the name of God,
giving life, bearing pain, making whole:

by the laying on of these hands
may the healing Spirit bless and support you,
for you are dearly loved;

by the laying on of these hands
may the healing Spirit flow freely in you and through you,
the power that is waiting to be set free among us,
that seeks our will and consent and trust;

by the laying on of these hands
may the healing Spirit confirm us in our faith,
making us strong together as one Body
in the service and friendship of Christ.

To each who receives the laying on of hands

N, through the laying on of these hands
and through our prayer,
receive the gift of the healing Spirit of God.

or

N, may the Holy Spirit,
the Giver of all Life and Healing,
fill you with Light and Love,
and make you whole;
through Jesus Christ our Saviour.

Anointing with Oil

[Some disease, either individual or corporate, does not go away. It would be cruel to raise a person's expectation that by a laying on of hands brain damage might suddenly be overcome or that years of emotional difficulty could suddenly evaporate as though they had never been. If severe damage has been done to an infant, physical or emotional or both, the road to deep healing takes time and is costly. In some ways it will be a way of a cross, a royal road maybe, but rough. Moreover, the goal is Christlikeness, and there were no legions of angels to rescue Jesus from pain and dying. He endured, but at what a cost.

We read in the Gospels of a woman of no great reputation who anointed Jesus with expensive ointment some days before his death. He received this gesture as a kind of consecrating of the way he was to go, the way of the cross and of burial. No one could share it with him, no one could share the moment of his dying and no one can share ours. But those around us who can see what is happening can support and bless and care.

It is here that we come to the old custom of anointing the sick with oil. Oil was a common medicine in the time of Jesus, and anointing the sick was a frequent practice in the life of the early Church. It is referred to in the Letter of James, 5.14. Centuries later the Venerable Bede of Jarrow wrote of the way in which oil that had been blessed in church was taken home by the people, where they administered anointing to one another. But by the twelfth century it had become "extreme unction", a ministry of anointing by the priest only, and only at the point of death.

However, that does suggest a connection with the anointing of Jesus for burial. The instinct may have been a sure one that linked such anointing with the kind of crisis that a person has to face alone.

Death is one obvious example. There comes the time of recognising the reality of imminent death, as when medical skill can do no more.

But a person may have to face a dark and lonely inner journey in order to understand and transform some compulsion or to be reconciled with the frightened, hurt, lonely child within who has been crying silently in the night for years.

Or we may ask for anointing that we may bear the lonely burden of a ministry of constant care for a schizophrenic son or a chronically ill mother or a deaf daughter.

We cannot follow one another into those places. There are depths which even the wisest cannot plumb. When someone we love is so suffering, we are like the disciples of Jesus in the Garden of Gethsemane. We cannot go with him in the struggle. The most we can do is to watch and pray. "I will be here for you, on the edge, and I may even fall asleep, but I will be here." The anointing with oil is for consecration on the way of one's truth, going through Gethsemane alone. To be anointed is to seek the courage to lay oneself open completely to the love and will of God, even if it involves a cup that you would prefer to pass by.

What can strengthen us in such circumstances is the faith that we shall touch no ground where Christ has not been. We have to go our own way of the cross, but the depths of pain and loss have been sounded for us. And in the midst of it we can sense Christ's sustaining presence. So the oil of anointing becomes the oil of gladness and rejoicing. Lamps are lit in the darkest of places, in the deepest dungeons of all, where maybe even Satan yearns to be again an angel of light.

And the one who suffers may be the one who heals us more than we realise. The trust and openness of the mentally handicapped may bring a grieving widow out of her isolation, and together they may know something of the peace that passes understanding. Little more can be said. We are on holy ground indeed. We reach the point in our prayers where we fall silent before a great mystery, that of suffering *redeemed*, not by magic, but by going through it until it yields to joy.

Jesus said very little after Gethsemane. His will was completely in tune with the will of the Father, and there was nothing more to say. The wordless cry with which he died on the cross carried our pains into joy. Perhaps those who watched could not tell at the time whether that cry was of pain or of joy—after all, the two cries sound very much alike. But Christian faith believes that there was both pain and joy, become one in resurrection life, whole and complete in the utter presence of God.]

Blessing of the Oil

Eternal and loving God,
bless this oil
and bless those who receive its anointing in trust,
that it may be to them
an eternal medicine,
a spiritual remedy,
an inward consecration,
to their strengthening, healing, and joy;
through Jesus Christ our Saviour.

Bidding to all

In the name of God,
who is great and good and love,
in the name of God,
giving life, bearing pain, making whole:

by this oil
may you be warmed and soothed,
and may the healing Spirit
penetrate the cells and fibres of your being,
that you may become whole,
giving thanks to God always and in all places,
and being ready to venture further on the way of faith;

by this oil
may you renew the consecration of your life
to the truth and service of God,
being not afraid to encounter God alone,
nor of dying in order to live
nor of bearing the burdens of those with whom you have to do;

know this oil
as a sign of gladness and rejoicing,
of lamps lit and of feasting,
of mirth and of joy.

To each who receives anointing

N, through faith in the power and the will
of our Saviour Jesus Christ
to make you whole and holy,
to consecrate you in his service with joy,
to give you courage
to go through the narrow gates of your journey,
I anoint you with oil
in the name of God,
who gives you life,
bears your pain,
and makes you whole.
Amen.

Personal Prayers During a Time of Corporate Silence

Spirit of God be
   within me to strengthen me,
   beyond me to attract me,
   over me to shelter me,
   beneath me to support me,
   before me to guide me,
   behind me to steady me,
   round about me to secure me.

Abba, I abandon myself into your hands . . . .
In your love for me do as you will . . . .
Whatever that may prove to be I am thankful . . . .
I am ready for all, I accept all . . . .
Let only your will be done in me,
   as in all your creatures,
   and I will ask nothing else . . . .
Into your hands I commend my whole being . . . .
I give myself to you with the love of my heart . . . .
For I love you, my God, and so I need to give,
   to surrender myself into your hands
   with a trust beyond measure . . . .
For you are my faithful Creator . . . .
May I indeed be your friend . . . .

[after Charles de Foucauld]

O God of the living,
in whose embrace all creatures live,
in whatever world or condition they may be,
I pray for those whom I have known and loved,
whose names and needs and dwelling place are known to you,
and I give you thanks for my memories of them.
In you, O God, I love them.
May this my prayer
minister to their growing and their peace;
in and through Jesus Christ
who broke the barrier of death
and lives for evermore.

[after John V. Taylor]

According to the riches of God's glory,
may we be strengthened with might
through the Spirit in our inner being,
and may Christ dwell in our hearts through faith,
that being rooted and grounded in love,
we may have power to comprehend with all the saints
what is the breadth and length and height and depth,
and to know the love of Christ which surpasses knowledge,
that we may be filled with all the fulness of God.

[Letter to the Ephesians]

Final Blessing

Receive a blessing
for all that may be required of you,
that love may drive out fear,
that you may be more perfectly
abandoned to the will of God,
and that peace and contentment
may reign in your hearts,
and through you may spread
over the face of the earth.

The blessing of God,
Giver of Life,
Bearer of Pain,
Maker of Love,
Creator and Sustainer,
Liberator and Redeemer,
Healer and Sanctifier,
be with you
and all whom you love,
both living and departed,
now and for ever.
Amen.

When Someone is Dying

A   Peace be to this house and all who live here.

A & B   We confess to God, who is all Love,
Father, Son, and Holy Spirit,
that we have sinned in thought, word, and deed,
and in what we have left undone.

A   The God of Love and Mercy
forgive you your sins,
and keep you in eternal life.
Amen.

A & B   Our Father, Who art in heaven,
Hallowed be Thy Name;
Thy Kingdom come,
Thy Will be done,
On earth as it is in heaven.
Give us this day our daily bread.
Forgive us our trespasses,
as we forgive those who trespass against us.
And lead us not into temptation,
but deliver us from evil.
For Thine is the Kingdom,
the Power and the Glory,
for ever and ever. Amen.

A   Through our prayer
and through the laying on of these hands,
may the Holy Spirit,
the Giver of all Life and Healing,
fill you, N, with Light and Love,
and make you whole;
through Jesus Christ our Saviour.
Amen.

A   Through this holy anointing
and through God's great love for you,
may the Holy Spirit move
in the depths of your being, N,
to make you whole and holy;
and may you be consecrated to God anew,
now and for eternity.
Amen.

Go forth upon your journey from this world,
in the name of God the Father who created you,
in the name of Jesus Christ who redeemed you,
in the name of the Holy Spirit who is sanctifying you.
May the angels of God greet you,
and the saints of God welcome you.
May your rest be this day in peace,
and your dwelling in the Paradise of God.

The Lord bless you and keep you,
the Lord make his face to shine upon you
and be gracious to you,
the Lord lift up the light of his countenance upon you,
and give you peace.

And the blessing of the God of Love,
Father, Son, and Holy Spirit,
be with you and all whom you love,
both living and departed,
now and for ever.
Amen.